CATS SET VII

CHARTREUX CATS

Kristin Petrie

ABDO Publishing Company

visit us at
www.abdopublishing.com

Published by ABDO Publishing Company, PO Box 398166, Minneapolis, MN 55439.
Copyright © 2014 by Abdo Consulting Group, Inc. International copyrights reserved
in all countries. No part of this book may be reproduced in any form without written
permission from the publisher. The Checkerboard Library™ is a trademark and logo of
ABDO Publishing Company.

Printed in the United States of America, North Mankato, Minnesota.
052013
092013

 PRINTED ON RECYCLED PAPER

Cover Photo: Photo by Helmi Flick
Interior Photos: Alamy pp. 17, 21; Glow Images pp. 7, 19; Photos by Helmi Flick pp. 5,
    11, 12–13; iStockphoto pp. 13, 15; Thinkstock pp. 8–9, 18

Editors: Rochelle Baltzer, Megan M. Gunderson
Art Direction: Neil Klinepier

Library of Congress Control Number: 2013932665

Cataloging-in-Publication Data

Petrie, Kristin.
 Chartreux cats / Kristin Petrie.
   p. cm. -- (Cats)
ISBN 978-1-61783-865-1
Includes bibliographical references and index.
1. Chartreux cat--Juvenile literature.   I. Title.
636.8--dc23
                                              2013932665

CONTENTS

Lions, Tigers, and Cats 4

Chartreux Cats 6

Qualities 8

Coat and Color 10

Size 12

Care 14

Feeding 16

Kittens 18

Buying a Kitten 20

Glossary 22

Web Sites 23

Index 24

Lions, Tigers, and Cats

Long ago, people would never have considered having a cat for a pet. After all, cats were wild! But over time, humans saw there were benefits to having these creatures around. They were impressive hunters! They kept **rodents** from invading stores of grains and other food.

Cats were finally **domesticated** more than 3,500 years ago. Tame cats were easier to keep around for their hunting skills. Calmer cats were also nice companions. Humans **bred** them to get qualities they desired in their new pets.

Today, there are more than 40 domestic cat breeds. Like lions and tigers, they all belong to the family **Felidae**. Some still have their wild looks and qualities. Others are beautiful, calm, and ready for showing. Still others, such as the Chartreux, are highly prized for their long and interesting history.

Chartreux *is pronounced "shahr-TROO."*

CHARTREUX CATS

The Chartreux is one of the oldest **domestic** cat **breeds**. Many historians believe the breed originated in what is now Syria. Legends tell of **Crusaders** bringing the cats back to French monasteries.

The Crusaders left the cats with Carthusian monks, which is where their name comes from. These prized mousers protected important papers from gnawing **rodents**. And, they killed snakes!

Others believe the Chartreux got its name from a fine Spanish wool. Animals were often named for their features. In this case, the breed's **dense**, woolly coat closely resembled the wool.

The Chartreux **breed**'s popularity spread through Europe in the early 1900s. Its population dropped during **World War II**, but fans of the breed saved it.

The breed first came to the United States in 1970. Today, it is a prized but somewhat rare pet and show cat. It was accepted for championship status by the **Cat Fanciers' Association** in 1987.

In the 1700s, the Chartreux was called "the cat of France."

QUALITIES

Chartreux are often called gentle giants. They are loving and calm. This easygoing character makes them good with children. They make nice family pets, but they will attach themselves to one person. These loyal cats will follow their favorite person constantly!

When not admiring their favorite person, Chartreux enjoy fetching, chasing, and other play. Many act more like dogs than cats! Chartreux are also very intelligent. Some respond to their names. And, they enjoy learning tricks. Chartreux have been known to open latches and push buttons.

Chartreux are quieter than some **breeds**. They make their needs known with soft meows. When

highly interested or entertained, Chartreux chirp!
They also have expressive faces, ears, and tails.

Chartreux get along well with other pets.

COAT AND COLOR

The Chartreux has a special and beautiful coat. In the cat world, its color is called blue. The Chartreux's coat comes in shades of gray from slate to ash. The ends of the hairs have a hint of silver.

The Chartreux's coat has two layers. The **dense** undercoat has a soft, plush feel. It helps keep the animal warm. The medium-short outer coat keeps out water.

Regular grooming is vital for the Chartreux. Many **breeders** suggest weekly combing. This helps avoid **matting** in the undercoat, especially when the cat **sheds** in spring and fall.

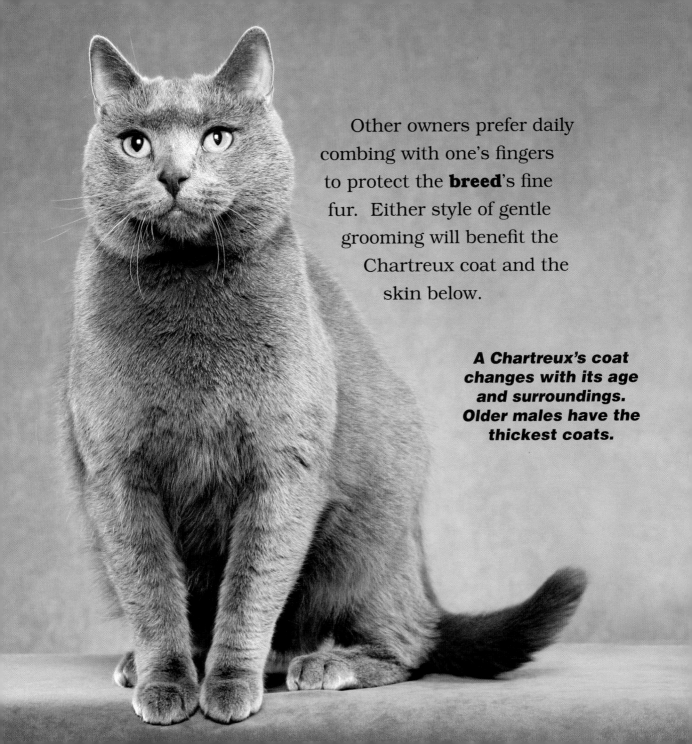

Other owners prefer daily combing with one's fingers to protect the **breed**'s fine fur. Either style of gentle grooming will benefit the Chartreux coat and the skin below.

A Chartreux's coat changes with its age and surroundings. Older males have the thickest coats.

SIZE

The Chartreux has a large, robust body. Wide shoulders support a full chest and large head. On average, males weigh 10 to 14 pounds (4.5 to 6.4 kg). Females are more often between 6 and 11 pounds (2.7 and 5.0 kg).

The Chartreux's head is round. It features tall, alert ears, full cheeks, and a narrow **muzzle**. Chartreux eyes are large and rounded. They are gold to deep copper in color. Brilliant orange is especially prized.

In contrast to its **hefty**, muscular body are the **breed**'s skinny legs. Many describe the Chartreux body as a potato on toothpicks! The fine-boned legs end in small, round paws. Last, the tail is moderate in length and slightly tapered at the end.

Some Chartreux have green eyes, but this is not allowed for show cats.

A Chartreux's muzzle curves up into a charming smile.

CARE

The Chartreux is easy to care for. These hardy cats suffer few health problems. Occasionally, a Chartreux has displacement of the kneecap. When mild, this **hereditary** condition is not of concern. If severe, it can be disabling.

Regular checkups at the veterinarian detect these and other health concerns. At the checkup, your cat will receive **vaccines** and an overall exam. The veterinarian can also **spay** or **neuter** cats that will not be **bred**.

At home, you'll need to provide additional care for your cat. Regular teeth brushing will prevent bacteria from collecting. Declawing is not advised for the Chartreux. Just trim its nails to prevent accidental scratching of family members. A scratching post will make scratching furniture less tempting!

Chartreux have quick reflexes and sharp senses.

FEEDING

Feeding your cat the right diet is another important part of caring for your pet. Like all cats, the Chartreux needs a balanced diet with enough protein.

High-quality cat foods come in different varieties. Dry foods are a good option because they do not spoil. And, they help clean your cat's teeth.

Some cats prefer moist food. This variety is perishable once opened. So, remove uneaten food promptly to prevent illness. Semimoist food is another option. Like dry food, it does not need to be refrigerated.

Chartreux cats are prone to weight gain. This is especially true for older cats. If concerned about your cat's weight, talk to your veterinarian about a special diet.

One thing that never changes is your cat's need for water. It helps maintain the Chartreux's coat and energy level. So, provide fresh water at all times.

Look for cat foods labeled "complete and balanced." The right food will help keep your Chartreux healthy and maintain its plush coat.

KITTENS

Cats are ready to mate when they are between 7 and 12 months of age. After mating, female cats are **pregnant** for about 65 days. The average **litter** size is four.

Newborn kittens are nearly helpless. After 10 to 12 days, they can see and hear. By this time, each kitten's first 12 teeth have come in. At first, kittens drink their mother's milk. By six to seven weeks, Chartreux kittens are eating just solid foods.

Separation from their mother is best at 12 to 16 weeks of age.

18

This extra time helps the kittens develop socially. Chartreux kittens continue to develop for many months. They keep growing until around three years of age.

By about three weeks, kittens can walk around and explore.

Buying a Kitten

The Chartreux **breed** is suitable for people young and old. These easygoing and independent cats don't need constant attention. They like to observe whatever is going on around them. But, they do love and need some attention.

Therefore, consider how much time you can give your pet. In addition, **domestic** cats live many years. Before adopting, ask yourself if you are ready for a commitment of ten or more years!

If you decide to bring home a Chartreux, find a reputable breeder. Good breeders know and provide the health history of their cats. They have properly **vaccinated** their cats and adapted them to life with humans.

Chartreux do not like to be carried. But, they will happily sit with their favorite people.

The Chartreux is relatively rare, so you may be put on a waiting list. During your wait, get some supplies! Quality food, a **litter box**, a scratching post, and grooming tools are a good start. Find a knowledgeable local veterinarian. Then you'll be ready for the new, loving addition to your family!

GLOSSARY

breed - a group of animals sharing the same ancestors and appearance. A breeder is a person who raises animals. Raising animals is often called breeding them.

Cat Fanciers' Association - a group that sets the standards for judging all breeds of cats.

Crusader - a person who participated in the Crusades. The Crusades were Christian military expeditions from the 1000s to the 1200s to reclaim the Holy Land from the Muslims.

dense - thick or compact.

domestic - tame, especially relating to animals. Something that is domesticated is adapted to life with humans.

Felidae (FEHL-uh-dee) - the scientific Latin name for the cat family. Members of this family are called felids. They include lions, tigers, leopards, jaguars, cougars, wildcats, lynx, cheetahs, and domestic cats.

hefty - heavy or bulky.

hereditary - passed down from earlier generations.

litter - all of the kittens born at one time to a mother cat.

litter box - a box filled with cat litter, which is similar to sand. Cats use litter boxes to bury their waste.

mat - to form into a tangled mass.

muzzle - an animal's nose and jaws.

neuter (NOO-tuhr) - to remove a male animal's reproductive glands.

pregnant - having one or more babies growing within the body.

rodent - any of several related animals that have large front teeth for gnawing. Common rodents include mice, squirrels, and beavers.

shed - to cast off hair, feathers, skin, or other coverings or parts by a natural process.

spay - to remove a female animal's reproductive organs.

vaccine (vak-SEEN) - a shot given to prevent illness or disease.

World War II - from 1939 to 1945, fought in Europe, Asia, and Africa.

WEB SITES

To learn more about Chartreux cats, visit ABDO Publishing Company online. Web sites about Chartreux cats are featured on our Book Links page. These links are routinely monitored and updated to provide the most current information available.

www.abdopublishing.com

INDEX

A
adoption 20

B
body 12
breeder 10, 20

C
Cat Fanciers'
    Association 7
character 8, 9, 20, 21
claws 14
coat 6, 10, 11, 17
color 10, 12

E
ears 9, 12
eyes 12

F
Felidae (family) 5
food 16, 18, 21
France 6

G
grooming 10, 11, 21

H
head 9, 12
health 14, 16, 20
history 4, 5, 6, 7
hunting 4, 6

K
kittens 18, 19

L
legs 12, 14
life span 20
litter box 21

M
muzzle 12

N
neuter 14

P
paws 12

R
reproduction 18

S
scratching post 14,
    21
senses 18
shedding 10
size 12
skin 11
socialization 19, 20
spay 14
Syria 6

T
tail 9, 12
teeth 14, 16, 18

U
United States 7

V
vaccines 14, 20
veterinarian 14, 16,
    21
voice 8, 9

W
water 17
weight gain 16